Living in the south west of England, we are [...]
range and quality of food on our doorstep. [...]
poultry, fresh vegetables from local farms, fis[...] from the
sea, wonderful cheeses and even wine are all now readily available,
if you know where to look. There has never been a better time for
gastronomes to eat sustainably!

Think global, act local, is not just a familiar catchphrase, it's what
this book is really about. Decisions we make in our lives can affect
our neighbours, whether they are next door or the next continent.
Climate change will be a huge challenge for us and for our children
for decades to come. Its effects will be felt most in the countries
where WaterAid works – in Africa, Asia and the Pacific region. We
have always been proud to support WaterAid and by buying this
book you are helping some of the world's poorest people gain
access to clean, safe water – something that will become ever more
important as temperatures rise.

We can all help to reduce the effects of climate change by doing
simple things like using public transport and saving energy. By
buying locally-produced food you can save 'food miles' and reduce
your own carbon footprint – enjoy the fresh tastes too.

As well as the famous chefs who have contributed, I'm very
pleased that many of our staff here at the Environment Agency
have supplied their own favourite recipes for the book. It's full of
inspiring ideas for dishes that you can make and places to find
those local ingredients. I hope you'll enjoy trying them out.

If you'd like to find out more about how WaterAid work, why not
visit their website at www.wateraid.org

Richard

Richard Cresswell
Regional Director
Environment Agency
May 2008

Environment
Agency

This book brings together two great passions – a celebration of the great food of the West Country and a desire to help some of the world's poorest people gain access to the most basic of needs – safe water and sanitation.

These essential services are crucial for life – but over one billion people live without safe water and over 2.5 billion lack sanitation. By buying this book and supporting WaterAid you are helping to change this, enabling communities around the world to gain access to safe water, sanitation and a healthier, brighter future.

We are very honoured to have contributions from some of this country's most talented and creative chefs alongside recipes from WaterAid staff and supporters. By coming together in this way we are not only sharing in the preparation and enjoyment of good food, but we are acknowledging the need to eat wisely while caring for the environment and each other.

Thank you all for buying this book and to everyone involved in its production; especially Jessie Burgess and the Environment Agency in the South West.

Barbara Frost
Chief Executive
WaterAid
April 2008

✔**WaterAid**

BREAD, CAKES & SNACKS

banana & walnut bread	6	fruity french toast	8
wholemeal malted seed bread	6	chocolate cake with luscious icing	9
tomato raisin loaf	7	yoghurt cake	10
gluten-free fruit loaf	7	heavy cake	10
'healthy' flapjacks	8	traditional cornish saffron buns	10

SOUPS

cornish blue cheese & cauliflower soup	12	spinach and asparagus soup	13
creamy leek soup	12	nigerian gbegiri soup	14
squash & swede soup	13		

MEAT DISHES

MICHAEL CAINES' roasted gressingham duckling with honey spices, savoy cabbage, celeriac and roasted garlic	16	toad-in-the-hole with bacon	19
		ghanaian hkatenkwan (groundnut stew)	20
		garlic chicken with cucumber	20
autumn sausage casserole	18	saucy liver	21
shepherd's pie	18	simple chilli con carne	21
somerset stew	19		

FISH DISHES

JAMES TANNER's seared scallops with smoked salmon and champagne sauce	24	creamy clouded yellow mussels	27
RICK STEIN's steamed mussels with tomato and tarragon	25	**PAUL DA-COSTA-GREAVES'** marinated wing of skate with crushed potatoes, cut tomatoes, chilli pesto and white wine reduction	28
spicy mackerel fish cakes	26	**PAUL DA-COSTA-GREAVES'** kombucha!	29
trout kedgeree	26	dogfish with leek fondue	30

MEATLESS DISHES

mushroom pearl barley risotto	32	tricolour champ	34
carrot flan	32	red cabbage	34
zambian nshima	33	unfailable ratatouille	34
zambian ndiwo	33		

PUDDINGS

JAMES TANNER's citrus soufflettes	36	lemon meringue ice cream	38
raspberry & white chocolate cheesecake	37	syrup apple sponge pudding	38
devonshire junket	37	orange coffee nectar	38
chocolate mousse	37		

PRESERVES

date & marrow chutney	40	green tomato chutney	40
mexican chutney	40	lemon curd	40

Why buy locally?

For all of the recipes in this book, you should be able to get most of the ingredients from local producers, but why is this so important?

- Buying from small local producers means you can find out more about how the food on your plate was produced.

- You can also try out varieties of fruit and vegetables and animal breeds that you'll never find in a supermarket, and you'll be supporting local producers and keeping money in the local economy.

- You'll also reduce the distance your food travels before it reaches you (food miles), cut down on wasteful packaging, and there's nothing like getting to know your local butcher, fishmonger or farmer, so they'll save you the best bits!

But not everything local is necessarily ethically produced. It's good to be aware of where and how your food is produced. Eggs can be local, but are they free-range?

If you have the time, shopping for groceries can be great fun, using farmers' markets, greengrocers and farm shops. Or you can try your hand at growing your own! And if you don't have time, many local producers now offer online ordering and deliveries (and a van run uses less CO_2 than single car journeys).

For the things you can't get locally – chocolate, exotic fruits, coffee – it's best to buy 'fair trade', so that the producers get a good price.

BREAD, CAKES & SNACKS

banana and walnut bread

I was given this recipe years ago when I was on a student exchange to Alfred University in New York state – hence the 'cup'* measurements and the 'regular all-purpose flour'! However, it has always turned out very well for me and, somehow, impressive as it's nice and moist, very tasty and quite dense. Great for picnics.

butter or margarine	½ cup
sugar	1 cup
free-range eggs	2 *slightly beaten*
medium bananas	3 *mashed*
regular, all-purpose flour (plain)	1 cup – *sifted before measured or weighed*
salt	½ teaspoon
bicarbonate of soda	1 teaspoon
wholewheat flour	1 cup
hot water	⅓ cup
walnuts	½ cup *chopped*

Preheat the oven to 170°C / 325°F / Gas 3

Grease a 1kg/2lb loaf tin

Melt the **butter or margarine** in a small pan on a low heat then transfer to a mixing bowl.

Blend in the **sugar** and then mix in the **egg** and the mashed **banana** blending until smooth.

Sift the **all-purpose flour** again with the **salt** and the **bicarbonate of soda** and add this and the **wholewheat flour** to the mixture adding these dry ingredients alternately with the **hot water**, a little at a time.

Finally, stir in the chopped **walnuts** and transfer to the loaf tin.

Bake in the oven for 1 hour 10 mins or until a knife comes out clean from the mixture.

Serve in slices with butter.

RECIPE SUPPLIED BY VANESSA ASHTON

---

*Be wary if you intend to convert to more standard (metric) measures: a cup of liquid is about 240ml while a cup of margarine is approximately 225g; a cup of *unsifted* flour is only 125g but a cup of *sifted* flour is even less, about 110g.

wholemeal malted seed bread

malt extract	2 tablespoons in warm water
dried yeast	1 teaspoon
vitamin C powder	¼ teaspoon
dried milk	2 tablespoons
oat bran	50g
strong white flour	200g
wholemeal flour	350g
salt	1½ teaspoons
raw cane sugar	1½ tablespoons
rapeseed oil	25ml
sesame seeds	mixture of your
pumpkin seeds	favourite seeds from
sunflower seeds	this list up to a
linseeds	maximum of 150g

This recipe is for bread made in a bread maker.

Dissolve the **malt extract** in about 150ml of hot water, then top up with colder water to 400ml to end up with the right quantity of 'warm' water. Set aside.

Add **all the other ingredients** (except the seeds) to the breadmaker in the order above, finishing off with the warm **malted water** – from dry ingredients to wet ingredients*.

Set the breadmaker to the wholemeal bread setting, making sure it is also set for a large loaf with a 'medium' colour if applicable.

Depending on the breadmaker, there will be a 'bleep' to indicate when to add the **mixed seeds** or there may be an automatic dispenser.

RECIPE SUPPLIED BY NIALL ALLSOP

---

*Be careful! Some breadmakers recommend the opposite, dry to wet … it doesn't really matter, the point is that the yeast and the water are kept as far apart as possible to prevent premature fermentation.

Why not try …
You can get the flour you need for these recipes from local mills like
Otterton Mill

gluten-free fruit loaf

cherries	40g *washed & dried*
sultanas	75g
butter	110g *softened*
caster sugar	110g
free-range eggs	2 large
ripe bananas	3 large *mashed*
fine rice flour	175g
cornflour	50g
gluten-free baking powder	2 teaspoons
salt	½ teaspoon

serves 8

Preheat the oven to 180°C / 350°F / Gas 4

Line a 1kg/2lb loaf tin or use 24 small paper muffin cases

Cut the **cherries** into quarters and mix with the **sultanas**. Set aside.

Cream the **butter** and **sugar** until pale, light and soft before adding the **eggs** one at a time; beat well after each addition and then add the mashed **bananas**.

Sift the **rice flour, cornflour, gluten-free baking powder** and **salt** together and fold carefully into the banana mixture.

Very gently stir in the **cherries** and **sultanas**, so that they are evenly distributed through the mixture.

Pour into the lined loaf tin and bake in the oven for between 1¼ and 1½ hours for the loaf; alternatively pour into 24 small muffin cases and cook for 25 minutes or until golden on top and a skewer inserted into the centre comes out clean.

Remove the loaf from the tin and cool on a wire rack; cool mini muffins on a rack in their paper cases.

RECIPE SUPPLIED BY AMANDA H JENKINS

tomato raisin loaf

butter	125g
caster sugar	175g
lemon rind	1 teaspoon *grated*
free-range eggs	2
tomatoes	240ml *skinned & chopped*
chopped raisins	80g
chopped nuts	30g
self-raising flour	175g *sifted*
wholemeal flour	60g *sifted*
mixed spices	1 teaspoon *sifted*
salt	¼ teaspoon *sifted*

Preheat the oven to 180°C / 350°F / Gas 4

Line the base of a 1kg/2lb loaf tin and grease well

Beat **butter, sugar** and **lemon rind** until creamy.

Add the **eggs** one at a time, beating well.

Press the **tomatoes** through a sieve to remove the seeds and add the pulp to the butter cream.

Add **raisins** and **nuts**.

Sift the **dry ingredients** over the tomato mixture and fold through.

Spoon into the loaf tin and bake for 35 to 40 minutes.

Remove from oven and allow to stand for 5 minutes before turning out onto a cake rack to cool.

Store in an air-tight container for 2 to 3 days before slicing.

RECIPE SUPPLIED BY JUDY BURNARD

'healthy' flapjacks

soft margarine	100g
golden syrup	4 tablespoons
porridge oats	225g
soft brown sugar	40g
raisins	60g

serves 8

Preheat the oven to 160°C / 325°F / Gas 3

Grease a shallow baking tray

In a pan, melt the **margarine** on a low heat with the **golden syrup**.

Remove from the heat and stir in the **oats**, **sugar** and **raisins**.

Pour the mixture into the greased baking tray and cook in the pre-headed oven for 30 minutes.

The raisins reduce the need for extra sugar ... experiment with nuts and other dried fruit.

RECIPE SUPPLIED BY RAY SMITH

fruity french toast

mixed fresh fruit	to taste *chopped*
banana	1 *mashed*
honey	1 dessert spoon
free-range eggs	2 *whisked*
sugar	2 teaspoons
bread	2 slices
butter	a knob
icing sugar	a pinch or two

serves 1

Chop the **fresh fruit** – kiwi, strawberries, raspberries, blueberries or any combination of these and/or others – and mash the **banana**. Mix the fruit and banana with the **honey***.

Whisk the **eggs** together with the **sugar**. Dip the **bread** in the eggs and allow the excess to drip off.

Place some of the fruit mix on one slice of bread, leaving a slight gap around the edge, and push the other slice down on top.

Melt a knob of **butter** in a medium hot pan and fry the sandwich on both sides until the bread is golden and slightly crispy.

Sprinkle with the **icing sugar** and spoon any left-over fruit on top.

Eat on its own or serve with ice cream or crème fraîche.

RECIPE SUPPLIED BY AMY PARFITT

---

*If you are feeling brave, mix a few dried chilli flakes into the fruit mix.

chocolate cake with luscious icing

For the cake	
self-raising flour	225g
cocoa powder	4 level tablespoons
margarine	225g
caster sugar	225g
vanilla essence	1 teaspoon
free-range eggs	4 medium
milk	2 tablespoons
golden syrup	60g

For the icing	
icing sugar	125g
cocoa powder	40g
butter	60g
water	3 tablespoons
caster sugar	80g

Preheat the oven to 150°C / 300°F / Gas 2

Grease the cake tin or tins. It's best to use two medium-sized tins, one for each layer of the cake.

Sift the **flour** and **cocoa powder** into a big mixing bowl.

Measure and add all of the remaining **cake ingredients** into the same bowl. Mix for several minutes with an electric hand mixer until the mixture is light and fluffy (you can do this by hand, but it will take longer).

Spoon the mixture into the tins – an equal amount in each. To create a flat top on one of the cakes (this will be the bottom layer), hollow out the middle slightly so that it is a little lower than the edge.

Place the tins in the oven and cook for between 30 and 40 minutes. Test them by prodding the top gently – if it springs back, it's done.

Leave the cakes to cool for a few minutes before turning them out onto a cooling rack.

Did you know that ...?
You don't have to buy sugar products, such as the caster sugar and syrup in this recipe, from sugar cane grown abroad. Silver Spoon produce sugar products like these using UK-grown sugar beet.

For the icing sift the **icing sugar** and **cocoa powder** into a mixing bowl.

Put the **butter**, **caster sugar** and **water** into a saucepan and cook over a medium heat. Keep stirring the mixture until the butter has melted and the sugar has dissolved and the liquid is clear and syrupy.

Bring to the boil and then remove immediately from the heat and pour straight into the bowl with the icing sugar and cocoa. Stir it in very quickly and keep beating it until the mixture is chocolate-coloured and shiny in appearance.

The cake should be iced straight away because the icing will dry out and go thick quite quickly. If it is too thick, add a little water until the consistency is right.

Pour a little less than half the icing onto the bottom layer, spread it across and place the other layer on top; pour most of the remaining icing onto it.

Using a palette knife, spread the icing across the top and onto the sides of the cake. (Have a bowl of hot water handy to dip the knife into if the mixture starts to dry out – the hot knife will melt the icing slightly and make it easier to spread.)

Once the whole cake is iced, add any decoration and then leave to set.

RECIPE SUPPLIED BY BEN VIZARD

9

yoghurt cake

fruit / plain yoghurt	125g pot
*vegetable oil	1 yoghurt pot
sugar	2 yoghurt pots
self-raising flour	3 yoghurt pots
free-range eggs	2

serves 8

Line the base of a 1kg / 2lb loaf tin

Empty the **yoghurt** into a mixing bowl.

Using the empty yoghurt pot as a measure, add the **oil**, **sugar** and **flour** and mix after each addition; add the **eggs** and mix well.

Pour the mix into the prepared loaf tin.

Cook for about 1½ hours from a cold oven set at 170°C; to test if it's done, insert and withdraw a knife – if it's clean, it's done and, if not, try again in 10 minutes.

Fresh fruit (blackberries, banana, apple, plum cherries …) can be added to the mix but this will add to the cooking time. And, of course, you can cook more than one at the same time.)

<small>RECIPE SUPPLIED BY ROBERT HARWOOD</small>

---

*If cholestrol is a problem then use rapeseed oil ... this is by far the best for reducing your cholestrol level

heavy cake

plain flour	450g
lard	110g
margarine	110g
sugar	110g
dried fruit	225g

Preheat the oven to 175°C / 325°F / Gas 3

Grease a shallow baking tray

Rub together **all the ingredients**, adding enough cold water to make a dough; roll to about ½-inch thick.

Put on baking tray, brush with water and mark with a knife.

Bake in a pre-heated oven for 15 to 20 minutes; remove and sprinkle with granulated sugar.

<small>RECIPE SUPPLIED BY ANN HARRISON</small>

traditional cornish saffron buns

saffron	1 sachet
caster sugar	110g
yeast	3 level tablespoons
plain flour	800g
lard	55g
margarine	55g
salt	½ teaspoon
currants	110g
sultanas	110g
free-range egg	1
lukewarm milk	425ml

Chop the **saffron** into small pieces and pour on a little boiling water; leave overnight to soak.

Mix the **yeast** with a little of the **sugar** and put it to one side in a warm place.

Meanwhile rub the **lard** and **margarine** into the **flour** and stir in the **currants**, **sultanas**, **salt** and remaining **sugar**.

Beat the **egg** and **milk** together and stir in the saffron and the yeast (which should now be starting to bubble) and gradually mix into the dry ingredients to make a firm dough.

Cover with a cloth and put in a warm place to prove.

In an hour the mixture should double in size. Knead it and cut into buns.

Leave it to stand for 30 minutes during which time the buns will rise again.

Preheat the oven to 220°C **and b**ake for 10 to 15 minutes.

<small>RECIPE SUPPLIED BY JUDY BURNARD</small>

SOUPS

cornish blue cheese and cauliflower soup

butter	25g
onion	1 medium *chopped*
garlic	1 clove *crushed*
vegetable stock	1 litre
cauliflower	1 large *trimmed*
Cornish blue cheese	50g
crème fraîche	2 tablespoons
salt & pepper	to taste

serves. 4

To make your own stock, trim the cauliflower into small florets and set aside. Place the stalk and leaves in a medium sized pan, add 1.5 litres of water and two bay leaves. Cover and bring to the boil and simmer for 20 minutes; strain the stock and set aside.

Melt the **butter** in a pan over a low heat, add the **onion** and **garlic** and cook for 3 to 5 minutes, until they become soft and clear.

Add the **stock** and **cauliflower florets** and simmer for 30 minutes or until the cauliflower is tender.

Blend the soup in a food processor or liquidiser until smooth then return it to the pan on a low heat.

Stir in the **cheese** until it melts then stir in the **crème fraîche** (or double cream) – ensure the soup does not boil after the crème fraîche (or cream) has been added. Taste and season with salt and pepper if necessary

Serve the soup in warm bowls with freshly baked crusty bread.

If you want to freeze this soup, do so before adding the crème fraîche – this can be added when the soup has defrosted and is being reheated.

Cornish Blue cheese is made by The Cornish Cheese Co. www.cornishcheese.co.uk

Recipe supplied by Sally Berridge

creamy leek soup

leeks	4 medium *finely diced**
butter	75g
plain flour	2 tablespoons
vegetable stock	1 litre
fresh cream	50ml
cheddar cheese	50g *grated*
black pepper	to taste *freshly ground*

serves 3 to 4

Sauté the prepared **leeks** in the **butter** until tender and slightly transparent.

Add the **flour** and stir continuously for 3 to 4 minutes.

Add the **stock** and bring to the boil; simmer for 20 minutes, stirring occasionally.

Strain and retain both the soup and the strained leeks.

In a food processor, purée half the strained leeks.

Put the remaining leeks, the puréed leeks and the soup back into the pan and add the **cream**, the **cheese** and the **black pepper** to taste.

Reheat and stir until the cheese has melted.

Serve with fresh crusty bread rolls.

Recipe supplied by Jonathan Burgess

*About 150g of prepared leeks.

squash and swede soup

olive oil	1 dessertspoon
onion	1 *chopped*
celery	2 sticks *chopped*
mixed herbs	1 teaspoon
butter	a knob
cardamom seeds	½ tablespoon *crushed*
swede	1 *peeled & diced*
butternut squash	1 *peeled, deseeded & diced*
salt & pepper	to taste
honey	2 tablespoons
chicken stock	approx 500ml
double cream	150ml
grated nutmeg	to taste
serves	*4*

Heat the **olive oil** in a pan and cook the chopped **onion** and **celery** until browned.

Mix in the **herbs, butter** and **cardamom seeds** before adding the **swede**, the deseeded **squash**, the **honey** and the **salt & pepper**.

Put the lid on the pan and leave on a low heat for 20 minutes.

Add enough **chicken stock** to cover the swede and squash and bring to the boil.

Once boiling, add the **double cream**.

Blend and sieve the soup; serve immediately with some **grated nutmeg** on top.

RECIPE SUPPLIED BY CLAIRE PANNETT

spinach and asparagus soup

onion	1 large *chopped*
garlic	3 cloves *finely diced*
carrot	1 large *chopped*
green beans	150g *chopped*
asparagus	1 packet *tailed & chopped*
rapeseed oil	1 tablespoon
spinach	450g* *chopped*
chillies	2 green and 1 red *deseeded & diced*
vegetable stock	750ml
low fat coconut milk	400ml (1 tin)
seasoning	to taste
serves	*4 to 6*

Prepare the first **five ingredients**; heat the **oil** in a pan then add the **vegetables** and sauté for 5 minutes

Add the **spinach** and **chillies** and cook for another 5 minutes.

Add the **stock** and bring to the boil. Cover, reduce the heat and simmer for 30 minutes.

Roughly purée and return to the pan; allow to cool a little before adding the **coconut milk** and **seasoning**. Reheat but do not let boil.

RECIPE SUPPLIED BY KAY BOWEN

*Growing your own spinach is really easy ... failing that, 450g equates to two supermarket packets.

nigerian gbegiri soup

black-eyed beans	600g
onions	3 medium *sliced*
dried thyme	¼ teaspoon
beef	2kg *cubed*
garlic	1 clove *crushed*
ginger	25mm long *grated*
black pepper	1 teaspoon
salt	to taste
crayfish	200g
ground pepper	1 teaspoon
stock cubes	2 *crumbled*
palm oil	100ml

serves 4 to 6 as a main course

Wash the **beans** in clean water, then soak in fresh water for about 5 minutes (any longer and they will be more difficult to peel).

Peel the beans skin by packing the beans in your palms and rub each palm full together to get the beans skin off.

Rinse peeled beans until thoroughly clean and put in a saucepan with one of the sliced **onions**, the **thyme** and some water and cook until tender.

Meanwhile wash the **beef**, drain and pat with kitchen paper.

Make a spice paste with about 50ml of water, the **garlic**, **ginger** and **black pepper** and half a sliced **onion**; add **salt** to taste.

Marinade the beef in the spice paste for 10 minutes then add another 30ml of water and cook until tender.

Drain the water out of the cooked and tender beans, pour into a bowl, mash to a smooth paste and pour into the cooking beef, add the rest of the **onions**.

Bring to the boil and simmer for 3 minutes.

Add the **pepper**, **crayfish** and **stock cubes** and allow to simmer for a further minute.

Add more water (about 100ml depending on how thick you want the soup) and the palm oil; stir until the oil is mixed through and add salt to taste.

Allow to simmer for 2 minutes.

RECIPE SUPPLIED BY CHIDINMA OBO, WATERAID IN NIGERIA

MEAT DISHES

Michael Caines

You can either use the excellent and tasty Gressingham duckling or, if you prefer, wild duck or mallard when in season (September until February).

The key to this dish is the sauce that has a sweet and tart character, made with honey and sherry vinegar. This helps to cut through the richness of the dish. The Chinese five spice mixed with the honey adds a touch of Asian flavouring that lifts the dish into another dimension.

Celeriac is one of my favourite root vegetables with its soft texture and a unique flavour that is intensified by the roasting. Make sure you blanch the garlic three times as indicated, so that you end up with a milder flavour of garlic. Winter garlic tends to be stronger than in the summer.

The secret to making the duck skin crispy is to score the skin before cooking it skin-side down, allowing the fat to render out during cooking.

roasted gressingham duckling with honey spices, savoy cabbage, celeriac and roasted garlic

serves 4

duck breast	4 x 180g
duck sauce	*see below*
Savoy cabbage	*see below*
celeriac	20 x 15mm dice *blanched in the fryer at 150°C until soft*
garlic	20 cloves *blanched 3 times and roasted*
clear honey & Chinese five spice	

Duck Sauce	
duck carcasses	1kg *chopped small*
Chinese five spice	5g
onion	1 large *cut into thick rings*
garlic	½ head
fresh thyme	15g
chicken stock	700ml
sherry vinegar	50ml
clear honey	100g
veal glace	300ml
cream	50ml
white peppercorns	5g
salt	2g

BORN IN EXETER, MICHAEL CAINES IS ONE OF BRITAIN'S HIGHEST PROFILE CHEFS. HIS RESTAURANT AT GIDLEIGH PARK HAS BEEN AWARDED TWO PRESTIGIOUS MICHELIN STARS AND AND HE IS ALSO CO-FOUNDER AND DIRECTOR OF FOOD & BEVERAGE FOR ABODE HOTELS AND MICHAEL CAINES RESTAURANTS. HE HAS APPEARED IN TELEVISION SERIES SUCH AS THE GREAT BRITISH MENU, AND WAS AWARDED AN MBE IN 2006.

Roast the **duck carcasses** lightly in the oven. Just before they finish roasting, sprinkle the bones with the **Chinese five spices**. Remove the tray from the oven and place on top of the stove, add the **onions** and **garlic** and very lightly colour the onions, then add the **thyme**. Cool the bones and deglaze the pan with the **chicken stock**.

Separately in a saucepan make a gastric with the honey and vinegar. Heat the **honey** and bring to a rolling boil and cook for 3 minutes, but be careful not to burn it or the sauce will become bitter. Add the **vinegar** and reduce. Now add the **carcasses and chicken stock** to the gastric, along with the **veal glace**, **peppercorns**, **thyme** and **cream**.

Bring to the boil and skim off the scum, reduce to a simmer and cook out for 30 minutes. Strain through a colander and then pass through a fine sieve. Reduce to a sauce consistency; adjust the seasoning and the acidity.

Savoy cabbage		
raw Savoy cabbage	350g	*sliced*
shallots	4g	*finely chopped*
butter	20g	
smoked back bacon	40g	*diced*
garlic purée	20g	
salt	to taste	
black pepper	to taste	*fresh ground*

Cook the **cabbage** in boiling salted water, then refresh in iced water. Drain well and pat dry.

Sweat the finely chopped **shallots** in the **butter**, then add the **smoked bacon**. Add the cooked cabbage and dry out before adding the **garlic purée**. Season with **salt** and **pepper** to taste.

Cooking the ducks

Refrigerate the ducks well before scoring the skins (we pop ours in the freezer for a few minutes). Taking a sharp knife score the fatty skin of the duck breast in a criss-cross pattern, but be careful not to cut the meat.

Season with salt and pepper and, using a thick, flat-bottomed pan, heat a little non-scented cooking oil and place the breasts skin side down. Cook at a fairly high temperature so that the skin renders out the fat, but be careful not to burn.

Once the skin is golden brown and crisp, turn the breast over and seal the other side for one minute before returning it once more to its skin side. Crisp the skin a little more before turning the breast onto its other side one more and finish cooking to your desired degree of doneness.

Once cooked remove from the pan and brush the **honey** and **five spice** over the crisp skin and leave to rest.

To serve

Place the **garlic** into a pan of cold water and bring to the boil, refresh in running cold water and repeat twice more. Now place the garlic into a thick bottomed pan with a little butter and season with salt and pepper. Cook slowly until lightly golden. Once the garlic is golden brown and soft, add the blanched **celeriac** into the pan to reheat.

Reheat the duck in the oven for a few minutes, and then slice thinly. Place the cabbage down the middle of the plate and dress the duck on top. Place five celeriac dice and pan-roasted garlic around the outside of the duck and then sauce.

somerset stew

local stewing beef	500g *cubed*
plain flour	1 tablespoon
olive oil	1 tablespoon
onion	1 *roughly chopped*
carrots	2 large *thickly sliced*
parsnips	2 *thickly sliced*
mushrooms	12 *halved*
beef stock	250ml
Guinness	1 bottle
red wine	a splash
fresh thyme	a few sprigs
bay leaf	1
salt & pepper	to taste
cornflour	*if required*

serves 4

Preheat the oven to 180°C / 350°F / Gas 4

Coat the **beef** in the seasoned **flour** and fry quickly in batches in the **olive oil** to brown on all sides; set aside.

Fry the **onions** till soft and then add the rest of the **vegetables** and fry for a few minutes.

Add the browned beef and add some **stock**, a splash of **red wine** and most of the **Guinness** – enough to just cover the ingredients.

Turn up the heat and bring to the boil, add a few sprigs of **thyme** and a **bay leaf** before **seasoning**.

Cover and put in the oven for 2 to 3 hours, checking occasionally on the liquid level – top up with stock, red wine or Guinness if required.

*Add some **cornflour** at the end if thickening is required.*

Serve with mashed potatoes and green beans.

RECIPE SUPPLIED BY SARAH BARDSLEY

shepherd's pie

potatoes	700g *cut up*
lard/sunflower oil	1 tablespoon
onions	2 *roughly chopped*
garlic	2 cloves *crushed*
*lamb or mutton	450g *minced*
stock cube or stock	1 cube or 60ml
butter	1 knob
pepper	to taste

serves 4

Cover the cut potatoes in lightly salted water and bring to the boil; cover and simmer for about 15 minutes.

Meanwhile, gently fry the **onions** (white or red) and **garlic** in about a tablespoon of lard or oil (if using left-over cooked meat then, if available, use any dripping) until softened.

Stir in the **mince**, crumble the **stock cube** over and cook gently for five to ten minutes. If using stock add about four tablespoons (60ml) to moisten but don't allow ingredients to swim in it! Cover pan.

When potatoes are soft pour off the water, mash with a knob of butter and pepper to taste.

Transfer the meat and vegetables to an oven-proof dish and spread the mash over the top using a fork. Put in the oven at a medium temperature (170°C) near the top to brown for about 20 minutes.

Variations include:
- *for added taste and texture, mix in a couple of dollops of tomato ketchup;*
- *add other vegetables – sliced mushrooms, runner beans, peas or grated carrot – to the meat mixture and cook a little longer;*
- *mash cooked cauliflower or broccoli or fried onion into the potatoes;*
- *leaving the skins on the potatoes gives the mash a nutty flavour;*
- *use beef instead for cottage pie;*
- *grate cheese atop the mash – not for weight-watchers but great with beef.*

RECIPE SUPPLIED BY TRICIA CASSEL-GERARD

*This recipe uses left-over (cooked) meat; if using uncooked mince, sear it first and transfer to another container to keep warm. The onions and garlic can then be cooked in the residue fat from the meat.

toad-in-the-hole with bacon

local pork sausages	8
local bacon	4 rashers *diced*
onion	1 *chopped*
cooking apple	1 *chopped*
sage	1 teaspoon
batter mix	1 pack*

serves 4

Preheat the oven to 200°C / 400°F / Gas 6

Lightly oil an over-proof casserole dish

Fry the **sausages** until just turning brown.

In another pan lightly fry the prepared **bacon** and **onion**.

Off the heat, stir the chopped **apple** in with the bacon and onion before laying over the bottom of the oiled dish.

Place the browned sausages on top and sprinkle with the **sage**.

Mix the **batter** according to the instructions on the pack and pour over the sausages and other ingredients.

Cook in the oven for 30 minutes or until the batter raises and turns golden brown.

Serve with mash potatoes, runner beans and onion gravy.

RECIPE SUPPLIED BY RAY SMITH

---

*Make your own if you know how!

autumn sausage casserole

onion	1 large *chopped*
garlic	3 cloves *chopped*
pork sausages	6
red pepper	1 *chopped*
yellow pepper	1 *chopped*
courgette	1 *chopped*
tomatoes	6 *chopped*
local apples	3 *cored & chopped*
local cider	450ml
salt and pepper	to taste

serves 4

In a casserole pan fry the **onion, garlic** and brown the **sausages** – preferably these should be from local pigs, raised outdoors.

Add the **peppers, courgette, tomatoes** (which can be skinned if preferred) and **apples**.

Add the cider as stock and cook for at least 30 minutes in the oven (at 180°C) or on the hob.

Add **salt** and **pepper** to taste.

Why not try ...
To get the cider you need for this recipe, you could try a local orchard such as Helford Creek or Sheppy's Cider.

garlic chicken with cucumber

cucumber	450g *peeled & deseeded*
salt	2 teaspoons
groundnut oil	1 tablespoon
chicken breasts	450g *skinned & cubed*
garlic	1½ tablespoons *finely chopped*
spring onions	1 tablespoon *finely sliced*
light soy sauce	1 tablespoon
Shaoxing rice wine *or* dry sherry	1 tablespoon
chilli bean sauce *or* chilli powder	2 teaspoons
sesame oil	2 teaspoons

serves 4

Peel the **cucumber**, halve it and remove the seeds with a teaspoon before cutting it into 2cm – 3cm cubes.

To remove the excess moisture from the cucumber, sprinkle it with the **salt** and leave in a colander to drain for 20 minutes.

Cut the **chicken breasts** into 2cm – 3cm cubes and set aside.

Rinse the cucumber in cold running water and blot the cubes dry with kitchen paper.

Heat a wok or large frying pan until it is very hot and add the **groundnut oil** and, when it is very hot and slightly smoking, add the chicken cubes and stir-fry them for a few seconds.

Add all the other ingredients except the cucumber – **garlic**, **spring onion**, **soy sauce**, **rice wine** (or **sherry**) **chilli bean sauce** (or **chilli powder**) and **sesame oil** – and continue to stir-fryfor another two minutes.

Now add the cucumber cubes and keep stir-frying the entire mixture for another three minutes. Serve at once.

Recipe supplied by Taryn Clements; original recipe in *Illustrated Chinese Cookery* by Ken Hom (BBC books 1984), page125

ghanaian hkatenkwan (groundnut stew)

chicken	1 *cut into pieces*
ginger	3cm piece
onion	½
water	2 cups
tomato purée	2 tablespoons
peanut oil	1 tablespoon
onion	1 cup *chopped*
tomatoes	1 cup *chopped*
peanut butter	⅔ cup
salt	2 teaspoons
chilli	2 *crushed*
aubergine	1 medium *chopped*
okra	1 *chopped*

serves 6

Boil the **chicken** with the **ginger** and **onion** half, using about two cups **water**.

Meanwhile, in a separate larger pot, fry the **tomato purée** in the **oil** over a low heat for about five minutes. Add the chopped **onions** and chopped **tomatoes**, stirring occasionally until the onions are clear.

Remove the partially-cooked chicken pieces and put them and about half the tomato/onion broth, in the larger pot.

Add the **peanut butter**, **salt** and **chillis** and cook for five minutes before stirring in the **aubergine**. Continue cooking until the chicken and vegetables are tender.

Add more broth as needed to maintain a thick, stewy consistency.

Recipe supplied by Chidinma Obo, WaterAid in Ghana

saucy liver

plain flour	5 teaspoons
mixed herbs	1 teaspoon
mild chilli powder	½ teaspoon
*liver	225g cubed
cooking oil	
(un)smoked bacon	4 rashers chopped
onion	1 sliced
garlic	1 clove crushed
or garlic granules	1 teaspoon
mushrooms	110g sliced
tomato soup	1 x 415g tin
paprika	1 teaspoon

serves 4

Mix the **flour, mixed herbs** and **chilli powder** then coat the **liver**.

Heat some **oil** in a pan and add the coated liver. When this starts to cook add the **bacon** (smoked or unsmoked as preferred) and fry until brown.

While this is cooking fry the **onions, garlic** (if using garlic granules add later) and **mushrooms** in a little **oil** until soft then add to the pan of liver and bacon.

Mix well and continue to cook for a few minutes. Add all the remaining **flour/herb mixture** and stir well.

Add the **tomato soup, garlic granules** (if using instead of fresh garlic) and **paprika** and mix well.

Simmer on a low heat stirring occasionally for about 30 minutes or as long as it takes to cook some rice. Serve hot on a bed of rice.

For a lower calorie meal use a little less flour and a low calorie soup and use Frylite instead of cooking oil.

RECIPE SUPPLIED BY LESLEY HOOPER

---

*I prefer pigs' liver but any liver will do.

Why not try ...
To get the beef you need for this chilli recipe, you could try a local producer of red ruby beef such as Piper's Farm or Clannaborough Barton Farm.

simple chilli con carne

olive oil	1 tablespoon
onion	1 sliced
local minced beef	450g
red chillies	2 small diced
chilli powder	to taste
green pepper	1 sliced
chopped tomatoes	1 tin
stock cube	1 (optional)
kidney beans	1 x 400g tin drained
mushrooms	4-5 large sliced
salt & pepper	to taste

serves 4

Fry the **onions** in the **olive oil** and add the **mince** to brown.

Add the **chillies** and **chilli powder** and stir for 1 minute.

Add the **green pepper** and stir for 2 minutes.

Add the **tomatoes** and the **stock cube** (if using) and stir for 2 minutes.

Add the **kidney beans** and stir for 1 minute.

Add the **mushrooms** and stir for 1 minute.

Add **salt & pepper** to taste.

Leave to simmer for 30 minutes and serve on basmati rice.

RECIPE SUPPLIED BY PAUL SADLER

In 1999, hydrogeologist Geoff Bowen and friends planted a vineyard on the sandy marl which underlies the Budleigh Salterton Pebblebeds at Ebford near Topsham in East Devon. The success of this first community project led to further commercial plantings at Ebford in 2002 and directly on the Pebblebeds at West Hill in 2005 and 2006. This year a further eight acres of vineyards has been planted at Clyst St George close to Topsham.

Pebblebed became officially organic in 2005 and today has some 22 acres under vines. Wines from Pebblebed Vineyards are now in commercial production and have already gained considerable local and national attention. Pebblebed Rosé 2004 won a prestigious national Gold Medal at the English and Welsh Wine of the Year Awards in 2004. The 2005 vintages won highly commended and a bronze medal in national and regional competitions.

Pebblebed wines can be purchased directly on line from www.pebblebed.co.uk or from the Pebblebed wine cellar in Topsham by appointment. A number of local and regional reputable retailers and restaurants also stock Pebblebed.

FISH DISHES

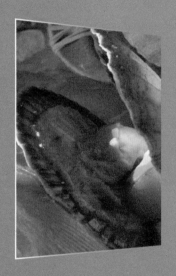

James Tanner

Champagne	250ml
shallot	1 *chopped*
whipping cream	125ml
unsalted butter	125g *cubed*
salt	to taste
smoked salmon	4 slices
olive oil	1 tablespoon
hand-dived scallops	16
salt and pepper	seasoning to taste
unsalted butter	20g
lemon	juice of half
rocket & watercress	to garnish

seared scallops with smoked salmon and champagne sauce

serves 4

In a saucepan, add the **Champagne** and chopped **shallot**. Reduce by three quarters.

Now place into a clean saucepan and add the **whipping cream**. Reduce by half and remove from the heat. Whisk in the cold **butter** until all the butter is melted. You should have a lovely velvety sauce. Season with **salt** and pass through a sieve. Set aside.

Lay the **smoked salmon** in the middle of the plates.

Place two frying pans on the heat. Add a little **olive oil** to each pan. The oil needs to be very hot. Season the **scallops** and then, very carefully, place in the pans. Add a little **butter** to each pan. Sear the scallops on one side for 30 to 40 seconds and then turn each one and repeat on the other side.

Squeeze **lemon** over all the scallops and transfer them onto a papered dish to drain.

Arrange the **rocket** and **watercress** in the middle of the smoked salmon. Place four scallops per person on the plate.

Gently warm the champagne sauce – DO NOT BOIL – as it will separate. Spoon the sauce around and over the scallops and serve.

JAMES TANNER AND BROTHER CHRIS HAVE ACHIEVED CELEBRITY STATUS DUE TO THEIR APPEARANCES ON *READY, STEADY, COOK* AND *SATURDAY KITCHEN* AS WELL AS THE SPECIALIST CHANNEL UKTV FOOD. THEY ALSO STARRED IN THEIR OWN SERIES *THE TANNER BROTHERS*. THEY OWN AND RUN THE TANNERS RESTAURANT IN PLYMOUTH, WHICH WAS NAMED AA RESTAURANT OF THE YEAR FOR 2007/08

Rick Stein

extra virgin olive oil	30ml
garlic	2 cloves *finely chopped*
mussels	1kg
dry white wine	30ml
unsalted butter	30g
tomatoes	60g *peeled, deseeded and finely chopped*
french tarragon	5g *finely chopped*
salt & black pepper	to taste

Make sure the mussels are tightly closed. If they are fresh-farmed ones there is no need to wash them, but if they are showing any signs of grit or sand wash them in copious amounts of cold water.

Take a large saucepan, add the **olive oil** and **garlic** and soften over a medium heat for about a minute.

Add the **mussels**, turn up the heat and add the **white wine**. Put a lid on the pan and cook for a few minutes until all the shells have opened, but only just. Stir the shells once or twice during the cooking to distribute them evenly. Remove and pour through a colander set over a bowl.

Keep the mussels warm while you transfer the liquor to a pan, heat until boiling, whisk in the **butter** then add the **tomatoes** and **tarragon**.

Check the seasoning; it's always a good idea to leave seasoning to the end with shellfish because you never know how salty they are going to be, then add **salt** if necessary and freshly ground black **pepper**.

Add the mussels back into the pan. Serve with plenty of crusty bread or alternatively with a mound of al dente linguine pasta.

steamed mussels with tomato and tarragon

serves 4

RICK STEIN IS AN INTERNATIONALLY-RENOWNED CHEF WHO CAME TO PUBLIC ATTENTION WITH HIS TV COOKERY SERIES *TASTE OF THE SEA* IN 1995. SINCE THEN HE HAS MADE NINE MORE. IN A LONG CAREER, RICK HAS COOKED TWICE FOR TONY BLAIR AT 10 DOWNING STREET, ONCE FOR THE FRENCH PRESIDENT JACQUES CHIRAC AND, ON ANOTHER OCCASION, FOR THE QUEEN AND PRINCE PHILIP TO CELEBRATE THE GOLDEN JUBILEE. HE WAS AWARDED AN OBE IN 2003.

trout kedgeree

brown basmati rice	100g (uncooked)
turmeric	½ teaspoon
paprika	½ teaspoon
ground coriander	½ teaspoon
ground cumin	½ teaspoon
chilli powder	¼ teaspoon
salt & pepper	to taste
leek	1 large *diced*
*trout fillets	350g *skinned*
bay leaf	1
free-range eggs	2 large
butter	a knob
low fat crème fraîche	150g
spring onions	2 *finely chopped*

serves 4

spicy mackerel
fish cakes

potato	500g *mashed*
butter	a knob
line-caught mackerel	125g (2 medium)
cider vinegar	a splash
cayenne pepper	to taste
Cheddar cheese	50g *grated*
spring onion	1 *finely sliced*

serves 4 as starter
serves 2 to 3 as main course

Cook and mash the **potatoes** with the **butter** until they are nice and fluffy.

Poach the **mackerel fillets** in a little water and **cider vinegar** for 2 to 3 minutes until the flesh is pale and flaky.

Skin and flake the poached fillets into a bowl, add the **mash, cayenne pepper, cheese** (a stong Cheddar or even Double Gloucester) and **spring onion**. Mix by hand and shape into balls.

Place the balls in a heated non-stick frying pan, squashing each down gently into a burger shape.

Fry for a couple of minutes on each side until golden brown, turning regularly.

Serve with seasonal local vegetables or salad.

<small>Recipe supplied by Jonathan Burgess</small>

Prepare and cook the **rice** as you normally do and time everything else accordingly. (You can also use refrigerated or frozen left-over rice.)

Mix the **five spices** with some **salt** and **pepper** and set aside.

Prepare the **leek** by topping and tailing, cutting lengthways and dicing; set aside.

While the rice is still cooking, put the **trout fillets** and **bay leaf** into a pan and cover with water; bring to the boil then turn down the heat immediately and poach, covered, for 5 minutes. Let stand for another 5 minutes.

At the same time, boil the **eggs** for 6 to 7 minutes in a small saucepan; drain, run under a cold tap and shell; cut each in half.

Flake the **poached trout** into a bowl; set aside.

Heat the **butter** in a pan and add the prepared **leek** and cook over a medium heat for 3 to 4 minutes. Stir in the **spices** and add the **cooked rice** and the **crème fraîche**; stir gently until everything is well coated.

Finally, add the **flaked trout** and continue to heat everything through for a few moments.

Serve, half an **egg** atop each serving, and a sprinkling of chopped **spring onions**.

<small>Recipe supplied by Kay Bowen</small>

---

*If you prefer a more robust flavour then use mackerel instead.

creamy clouded yellow mussels

mussels	1.35kg *cleaned of barnacles and beards*
butter	30g
onion	110g *finely diced*
coriander	handful *roughly chopped*
Clouded Yellow wheat beer	125 ml
double cream	150 ml
cracked black pepper	a good pinch

Serves 4 to 6

Wash the **mussels** under plenty of cold, running water. Discard any open ones that won't close when lightly squeezed. Pull out the tough, fibrous beards protruding from between the tightly closed shells and knock off any barnacles. Give the mussels another quick rinse to remove any little pieces of shell.

Soften the **onion** in the **butter** in a large pan big enough to take all the mussels – it should only be half full.

Add the **mussels** and **beer**, then turn up the heat to rapidly boil the beer for 5 minutes tossing the mussels around during cooking until all have opened.

Add the **cream**, **coriander** and **black pepper**; stir and heat through.

Then spoon into large warmed bowls and serve with lots of warm crusty bread, Cornish butter ... and a nice cold glass of Clouded Yellow from St Austell Brewery.

RECIPE SUPPLIED BY PAUL DRYE, CATERING DEVELOPMENT MANAGER AT ST AUSTELL BREWERY

marinated wing of skate with crushed potatoes, cut tomatoes, chilli pesto and white wine reduction

serves 4

Paul Da-

skate wings	4 x 175-220g *trimmed*
lime	1 *zested & juiced*
grapeseed oil	1 tablespoon
extra virgin olive oil	1 tablespoon
dry white wine	10ml
clarified butter	25g
milled sea salt	to taste
white pepper	to taste
local new potatoes	450g *washed*
white wine	15ml
cherry tomatoes	1 punnet
rosemary	1-2 small sprigs
chilli pesto*	4 tablespoons
fresh herbs	to garnish

*Chilli pesto – bought from any deli, supermarket or me! Alternatively buy a basic pesto and add ½ teaspoon of a de-seeded finely chopped red chilli.

PAUL DA-COSTA-GREAVES IS MASTERCHEF OF GREAT BRITAIN CO-OWNER & DIRECTOR OF THE GALLEY RESTAURANT TOPSHAM, DEVON. WHERE HE ALSO PRODUCES AND MANUFACTURES HIS RETAIL FOOD COMPANY 'FEEDING YOUR IMAGINATION LTD'. PAUL IS ALSO A SPIRITUAL HEALER & ALTERNATIVE THERAPIST. HE FOLLOWS A ZEN-STYLE APPROACH TO COOKING, AND HIS RESTAURANT IS REGARDED AS ONE OF THE FINEST FISH RESTAURANTS IN THE REGION.

Delicately score and cut into the flesh of the skate wings.

Into a medium-sized bowl marinade, for approximately 10 to 15 minutes, the **skate wings**, the **olive oil**, **grapeseed oil**, **butter**, **wine**, **lime zest & juice** and the **salt** and **pepper**.

Put the **new potatoes** into boiling salted water and cook until tender. Remove from the heat, drain and cool.

Grill the skate under a low/medium heat with a dash of grapeseed oil, a knob of butter and a dash of white wine, gently turning after approximately 10 minutes each side.

Place the potatoes between the palms of hands and crush gently. Into a non-stick saucepan, place the **crushed potatoes**, **chilli pesto**, quarter-cut **cherry tomatoes**, the **rosemary** and a few dashes of **white wine** and a **knob of butter**.

Warm through and and gently spoon the mixture onto plates.

Delicately rest the skate on the cut tomatoes and 'pesto' potatoes. Finish off with a little of the juices running off the fish. Garnish with fresh garden herbs

kombucha!

A magical explosion of delicately grilled fillets of turbot resting beautifully on a seaweed mash, garnished with chilli ice cream, seared scallops and masked with a snipped herb, ginseng & caviar butter sauce.

serves 4

jacket potatoes	5 medium-sized
un-salted butter	90g *melted*
egg yolk	1
spring onions	half a bunch *washed and finely chopped*
*dried mixed seaweed or fresh washed	25g *chopped*
fresh herbs	1 teaspoon *chopped*
fresh turbot fillets	4 x 175-220g *skinned*
extra virgin olive oil	1 tablespoon
grapeseed oil	1 tablespoon
vegetable stock	25ml
dry white wine	a dash
lime	zest and juice of half
milled sea salt	to taste
white pepper	to taste
water	50ml
dry white wine	50ml
vegetable stock cube	¼ pinch
**dried ginseng flakes	a pinch
un-salted butter	couple of knobs
chives	½ teaspoon *snipped*
salmon keta & avruga caviar	¼ teaspoon
large scallops	3 per person *peeled*
***chilli ice cream	12 small balls

For the mash boil the **potatoes** and simmer until cooked. Drain and mash together adding melted, **un-salted clarified butter**. Whisk together to fluff up, adding **egg yolk**, chopped **scallions (spring onions)**, seaweed and required **seasoning**. (it should not need salt as this will come naturally from the weed). Finally add chopped **herbs** and leave to one side, keeping warm.

Take the **turbot fillets** out of the fridge and leave to rest for 15 minutes.

Marinate with the **olive oil, grapeseed oil, clarified butter**, the dash of **wine, lime zest and juice, milled salt & white pepper** for 5 minutes.

Place the turbot onto a foiled oven tray and cook under a low/medium grill for approximately 15 minutes.

Pour the **water** and **dry white wine** into a small pan with **ginseng** and a small pinch of **vegetable stock**. reduce until it is about half its previous volume then add a couple of knobs of cold **butter** to the pan and swish around to create a light butter sauce. Add a good pinch of the snipped **chives** and the **salmon keta & avruga caviar**.

Place three peeled, large **scallops** per person (without the coral) into a hot non-stick frying pan without oil. Sear the scallops for approximately 20 to 30 seconds on each side. Gently season with milled pepper.

Remove the fish from under the grill and place onto the mash in the centre of a warm plate.

Dribble the warm sauce around the fish. Take the scallops and position around the mask in a triangle. Then take a small melon ball cutter and place three balls of chilli ice-cream between the scallops.

*Sea veg, sea lettuce duse or wakame can be bought from any health store or supermarket.
**ginseng – any good health shop, good for numerous health benefits
***Use Purbeck (Dorset) chilli ice cream or slightly melt any vanilla ice cream and mix in chopped red chillies and pop back in the freezer until required.

dogfish with leek fondue

mushrooms 100g
salted butter a knob
black pepper to taste

leeks 3 large *washed & sliced thinly*
lemon juice of half
sea salt ½ teaspoon

crème fraîche 1 pot
mustard 1 tablespoon
salt & pepper to taste

dogfish / huss 600g *prepared*
plain flour 4 tablespoon

shallots 4 *thinly sliced*
salted butter a knob
white wine 1 tablespoon

serves 4

Preheat the oven to 180°C / 350°F / Gas 4

Slice the **mushrooms** thinly and fry in the salted butter and ground black pepper.

Prepare the leek fondue (*fondue de poireaux*) by cooking the prepared leeks in a pan with a little butter. Add a pinch of **sea salt** and **lemon juice**, cover the pan, leave for a few minutes.

When the leeks have softened, add two tablespoons of **crème fraîche** (hold back four tablespoons), the **mustard** and the **salt & pepper** to obtain a thick mixture.

Wash the prepared **fish**, cut it into 12cm chunks and coat them in **flour**. Fry the sliced **shallots** for a minute in **salted butter** before adding the fish; fry until golden.

Add the cooked **mushrooms**, the **white wine** and the rest of the **crème fraîche**; season and leave for a few minutes on the heat.

Serve with the 'fondue de poireaux', some steamed new potatoes and a good white wine.

RECIPE SUPPLIED BY JULIE VERRÉ

Did you know that ...
Overfishing is a great threat to marine wildlife, and it's very important that we conserve our stocks of fish and sea-food. By going to www.fishonline.org you can find out more about which species of fish are endangered and what you can do to help preserve them.

MEATLESS DISHES

mushroom pearl barley risotto

unsalted butter	10g
shallots	4 *finely diced*
garlic	2 cloves *crushed*
pearl barley	350g
chicken / vegetable stock	1.1 litres
mushrooms	250g
parmesan shavings	to serve
fresh thyme leaves	1 teaspoon
cracked black pepper	to serve

serves 4

Melt the **butter** in a heavy-based pan.

Add the diced **shallots** and stir until soft then add the **garlic** and cook for a few minutes longer.

Add the **pearl barley** and the **stock** (or water) and stir thoroughly to ensure all the barley is covered with liquid.

Reduce heat and simmer for 30 minutes. The liquid will evaporate but to ensure the barley is cooked you may have to add a little more water if it all evaporates before the time is up.

Add the **mushrooms** (single variety or mixed) and continue to cook for a further 10 minutes.

Stir half the **parmesan** and the **thyme** through the risotto so the texture is slightly sticky.

Serve with plenty of **cracked black pepper** and the rest of the **parmesan** sprinkled over the top.

<small>RECIPE SUPPLIED BY LUCIE MARTIN</small>

carrot flan

wholemeal pastry	
wholemeal flour	225g
salt	1 teaspoon
butter	110g *cubed*
cold water	to mix
filling	
carrots	450g
free-range egg yolks	2
reduced cream	75ml
grated cheese	4 tablespoons
chives	3 tablespoons *finely chopped*
fresh rosemary	½ teaspoon *finely chopped*
salt & pepper	to taste

serves 4

Preheat the oven to 150°C / 300°F / Gas 2

Line a 20cm (8in) flan tin

Place the **flour** and **salt** into a mixing bowl; add the **butter** and rub in using finger tips until the mixture resembles breadcrumbs. Add the **cold water** gradually and mix in with a knife. Knead the dough lightly with a clean cool hand.

Roll out the pastry on the lined flan tin and bake 'blind' in the preheated oven for 20 minutes. Leave the oven on.

For the filling, cook and mash the **carrots** before beating in the **egg yolks**, **cream**, **cheese**, **chives**, **rosemary** and **salt & pepper**.

Spoon the mixture into the pastry case. Bake for 30 minutes or until the filling is firm.

Serve warm with a green salad.

<small>RECIPE SUPPLIED BY JUDY BURNARD</small>

zambian nshima

hot water	3 cups
cold water	1 cup
corn meal	2 to 3 cups

Bring three cups of **water** to the boil in a pan.

Meanwhile, make a paste using the **cold water** and some of the **corn meal**.

Add the paste to the boiling water and stir with a wooden spoon until thickened like porridge.

Cover and simmer for about 15 minutes then lower the heat a little, uncover and gradually add the remaining **corn meal**, stirring constantly and flattening any lumps that form.

Continue to add the corn meal and stir until the nshima thickens to the desired consistency – some like it thin and others prefer it thick.

Cover and reduce heat to its lowest setting and leave to cook for a few minutes; stir once again and serve in a slightly wet serving dish ... try it with a vegetarian ndiwo (see opposite).

zambian ndiwo

unsalted peanuts	1 cup *ground*
onion	1 *sliced*
tomatoes	2 medium *sliced*
water	as required
salt	to taste
spring greens / spinach	2 bunches *washed & chopped*

In a medium-sized saucepan, boil the **onion**, **tomatoes** and ground **peanuts** in a little **water**, adding **salt** to taste

After a few minutes add the chopped **greens**.

Stirring occasionally, continue cooking for 15 to 20 minutes until the peanuts are soft and the mixture has become a fairly thick buttery sauce.

Serve hot or cold.

For an extra kick, add a finely chopped red chilli!

RECIPES SUPPLIED BY WATERAID PROGRAMME STAFF – ZAMBIA

tricolour champ*

new potatoes	3 to 4 *halved*
sweet potato	1 *peeled & cubed*
rapeseed oil	1 dessertspoon or less
spring onions	2 *trimmed & chopped*
chilli flakes	a small pinch
mediterranean herbs	a small pinch
black pepper	to taste

serves 2

Put the **new potatoes** in a pan of cold water, bring to the boil and boil for 5 to 6 minutes before adding the prepared **sweet potato**; cook for a further 10 minutes.

Meanwhile prepare the **spring onions**, heat the **oil** in a small pan and add **all the other ingredients** and fry gently for 2 minutes.

Drain the potatoes (retaining some of the water), mash roughly (keeping it chunky) and add the cooked onion mixture and some of the cooking water if it's too dry.

Serve with anything and everything!

RECIPE SUPPLIED BY NIALL ALLSOP

---

*Champ is a traditional Northern Irish dish – basically mashed potatoes, creamed with butter, milk and scallions (spring onions). This version, by also using sweet potatoes with unpeeled new potatoes and *not* creaming the potatoes, is a much healthier option ... adding the chilli flakes and herbs gives it a really tasty 'bite'.

red cabbage
cooked in a 800w microwave

red cabbage	450g *shredded*
cooking apples	2 *peeled & sliced*
currants	60g
blackcurrant cordial	45ml
white wine vinegar	45ml
onions	60g *chopped*

Put **all the ingredients** in large bowl and cook in the microwave for 10 minutes at *high*.

Stir and test.

Freezes well, can be used hot or cold with salad.

RECIPE SUPPLIED BY DOROTHY DAVENPORT

unfailable ratatouille

vegetable oil	1 tablespoon
garlic	1 clove *crushed*
onions	2 medium *quartered & thinly sliced*
courgettes	4 large *halved & thinly sliced*
tomatoes	6 large *diced*
tomato ketchup	a good squeeze
Worcestershire sauce	sprinkle to taste
mixed herbs	a good sprinkle
salt & pepper	to taste
button mushrooms	6 *sliced*
Cheddar cheese	to cover top *grated*

serves 4 to 6

Heat the **oil** and **garlic** in a large frying pan and add the sliced **onions** and stir frequently.

Meantime slice the **courgettes** and add to the pan; stir till the mixture softens but does not turn brown.

Dice and add the **tomatoes** with any flesh or juice and mix in a good dollop of **tomato ketchup** and a good sprinkling of **Worcestershire sauce**

Stir and lower the heat before adding the seasonings and **mixed herbs**.

Turn on the grill to high

Slice the **mushrooms** and stir into mixture and then grate enough cheese to cover the dish and sprinkle over it.

Put the frying pan under the grill until the cheese is melted and just turning brown.

Eat immediately or store in the fridge to eat later.

RECIPE SUPPLIED BY SUE ALCOCK

Why not try ...
To get the cheese you need for this recipe, why not try some real cheddar cheese such as Wyke's Farm or the Cheddar Gorge Cheese Co.

PUDDINGS

James Tanner

plain flour	125g
sugar	15g
salt	a pinch
free-range eggs	2
milk	330ml *boiled & cooled*
double cream	100ml
sunflower oil	1 tablespoon
crème patisserie	70g
egg whites	2
sugar	a pinch
vanilla extract	a pinch
sugar	125ml
butter	125gm *cubed*
oranges	juice of 2
	rind of 1
	blanched till soft
lime	rind of 1
	blanched till soft
mandarin vodka	2 shots

citrus soufflettes

For the crêpes mix the **flour, sugar** and **salt** in a bowl. Add the **eggs** and whisk. stir in a third of the **milk** and beat through. Pour in the **cream** and then the remainder of the milk. Mix and rest for 1 hour.

Preheat the oven to 220°C

Warm a crêpe pan and lightly oil with **sunflower oil**. Pour a ladleful of the mixture into the pan and fry till golden brown; flip over and cook until golden. This takes about 2 minutes per side. Repeat the process, making four crêpes in all.

To make the soufflé filling, whisk the **egg whites** in a bowl to a soft peak, fold in the **crème patisserie** and **vanilla extract** with a pinch of **sugar**. Put this mixture in a piping bag. Fold pancakes in half then half again so they form triangles. Pipe in soufflé mix and bake for 2½ minutes in the oven.

To make the sauce heat the **sugar** and **butter** to caramel, add the **zest** and the **vodka**, stir in and add the **juice** and serve.

serves 2

raspberry and white chocolate cheesecake

gelatine	2 teaspoons
boiling water	50ml
digestive biscuits	200g *made into crumbs*
melted butter	50g
regular cream cheese	400g
caster sugar	150g
lemon rind	1 teaspoon *grated*
white chocolate	200g *melted*
cream	200ml *lightly whipped*
frozen raspberries	200g
fresh raspberries	as required
icing sugar	to dust

Dissolve the **gelatine** in the **boiling water** and set aside to cool.

Combine the **biscuit crumbs** and **butter** and press into base of greased 20cm springform tin.

Beat the **cream cheese, sugar** and **lemon rind** with an electric mixer until smooth.

Stir in the **gelatine mixture** and (good quality) **white chocolate** until smooth, then gently fold in the **cream** and **frozen raspberries** – you can freeze your own fresh raspberries but they must remain frozen for this recipe.

Pour the filling into the prepared base and refrigerate for 3 hours or until set.

Decorate with the remaining **fresh raspberries,** sprinkle with **icing sugar** and serve.

This cheesecake is very indulgent and is best eaten in small quantities!!!

Recipe supplied by Lucie Martin

devonshire junket

full cream milk	500ml
sugar	20g / 1 dessertspoon
rennet	30g
vanilla essence	to taste (about 2 tsps)
brandy *(optional)*	up to 40ml*
grated nutmeg	to taste
Devonshire clotted cream	125g (or more!)

Warm the **milk** until about 36°C (blood heat) – DO NOT BOIL.

Warm a pudding basin/trifle dish (or similar) to the same temperature and pour in the hot milk before adding the **sugar, rennet, vanilla essence** and **brandy** (if using).

Scatter **grated nutmeg** over the surface or decant into individual bowls and scatter nutmeg on on each.

Leave in a warm place for two hours to set, then refrigerate.

Serve when required with **clotted cream**.

Junket is the dish of Devon,
A better dish is hard to find,
This is everyone's opinion,
Excepting those who're out of mind.

Recipe supplied by Mark Rice, from an original recipe by Vera Rice

*Adding brandy is recommended by Mrs Beeton in her book on household management [entry 1,631]. Mrs B says of junket "Seasonable at anytime".

chocolate mousse

butter	60g
plain chocolate	225g
free-range eggs	4 *separated*
whipping cream	240ml

Heat chocolate pieces in a bowl over hot water.

Off the heat, beat in butter and the egg yolks; lightly whisk the egg whites until just holding shape, fold into chocolate.

Spoon into dishes and decorate with the cream.

Recipe supplied by Ann Harrison

lemon meringue ice cream

whipping cream	600ml
Greek yoghurt	225g
lemon curd	320g
lemons	juice and zest of 2
meringue nests	6 *broken up*

Whip the **cream** until fairly stiff then fold in the **yoghurt**.

Stir in the **lemon curd**, **lemon juice** and **zest**.

Add the broken **meringues** ... but make sure the pieces are not so small that they will dissolve into the mixture.

Put into a shallow container and freeze.

Put in the fridge for 40 minutes before serving.

RECIPE SUPPLIED BY KATE CAVILL

syrup apple sponge pudding
cooked in a 800w microwave

golden syrup	2 tablespoons
margarine	115g
caster sugar	115g
free-range eggs	2
self-raising flour	115g
bramley apples	2 *chopped & cooked*

Grease a 1½ pint basin.

Put the **syrup** in the basin.

Cream the **margarine** and **sugar** then add the eggs and beat.

Fold in the **self-raising flour** and the cooked **apple** and cover loosely with cling film

Microwave for 6 minutes at *medium*; test.

RECIPE SUPPLIED BY DOROTHY DAVENPORT

orange coffee nectar

This is a recipe with a history.

I first came across it in Sardinia where an elderly woman, living in a small hilltop village, gave me a bottle as a present.

Six months on and I was in need of a refill and headed back to Sardinia.

My 'source' had less than a bottle left and, despite my half-hearted protestations, insisted that we have half each ... and then, in a secretive Italian whisper, shared the recipe too.

I have been making it ever since but, until now, divulged it to few ... though I have long shared the end result with one WaterAid employee for whom it has become the beverage of choice.

Though not really a 'pudding' it is, like some puddings, more of a post-prandial indulgence!

oranges	2
coffee beans	80
grappa	around 2 litres
sugar	800g*

serves a purpose

Sterilise a 3-litre wide-necked Kilner-type jar and only buy oranges that will fit into the jar

With a sharp knife (I use a Stanley knife) make 40 cuts into each **orange** and push a **coffee bean** right in to each slit.

Pour about half the **grappa** into the jar, add the **sugar** and shake vigorously (with the top on!) till the sugar is almost dissolved.

Carefully add the bean-impregnated oranges and top up with as much grappa as the jar will take; seal and give another good shake.

Store in a cool cupboard for 40 days and shake every few days to dissolve all the sugar.

Remove the oranges, bottle and drink.**

RECIPE SUPPLIED BY NIALL ALLSOP

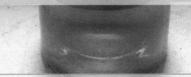

*If you like a really sweet liqueur, then add some more sugar (up to 1k).

**Be warned ... it is both heavenly and strong and also, in the nicest possible way, addictive!

PRESERVES

date and marrow chutney

marrow	3.6kg *peeled, deseeded & diced*
salt	225g
onion	1 large *finely chopped*
stoned dates	900g *chopped*
stoned raisins	225g
sultanas	225g
currants	110g
mustard powder	1 rounded teaspoon
brown malt vinegar	1 litre
granulated sugar	225g

makes 7lb chutney

Arrange the prepared **marrow** in a deep bowl sprinkling each layer with **salt**; cover with a tea towel and stand in a cold place overnight.

Drain the marrow well, discarding the liquid.

Mix the prepared **onion** and **dates** with the **raisins, sultanas** and **currants** in a large bowl; mix in the **mustard powder**.

Put **vinegar** and **sugar** in a large saucepan and heat gently until the sugar has dissolved.

Add the **marrow** and **dried fruit mixture** and bring to the boil; boil gently for 1¼ hours until thick then bottle and seal.

RECIPE SUPPLIED BY JUDY BURNARD

mexican chutney

avocado	1 *peeled & mashed*
chillies	2 *finely chopped*
cherry tomatoes	5 *chopped small*
coriander leaves	bunch *finely chopped*
garlic	1 clove *crushed*
red onion	½ *finely chopped*
lime	juice of 1

Mix all the prepared ingredients thoroughly. Keep in a plastic container with an air-tight seal (it may go dark if exposed to air for too long – a few drops of lime juice on the top, helps preserve the bright green colour).

Refrigerate for 2 hours; serve with anything!

RECIPE SUPPLIED BY ROBIN J LEIVERS

green tomato chutney

tomatoes	1.35kg *chopped*
onions	700g *chopped*
apples	450g *chopped*
vinegar	350ml
mustard seeds	60g
ground mace	½ teaspoon
cayenne pepper	¼ teaspoon
white pepper	½ teaspoon
salt	60g
sultanas	handful (optional)
cloves	a few
sugar	675g

Bring the prepared **tomatoes, onions** and **apples** and the **vinegar** to the boil and simmer for 1 hour.

Add all the **remaining ingredients** and simmer for a further 1½ hours.

Store in sterilised jars.

RECIPE SUPPLIED BY JIM GARLAND

lemon curd
cooked in a 800w **microwave**

lemons	2 – juice & *grated* rind
butter	60g
free-range eggs	3 *beaten*
granulated sugar	225g

Prepare the **lemons**.

Heat the **butter** for 1½ minutes at *high*

Add the **lemon juice & rind**, **sugar** and **eggs** and beat.

Cook uncovered for 5 minutes at *high*, stirring after every minute.

Pot and cover or freezes well in plastic containers.

RECIPE SUPPLIED BY DOROTHY DAVENPORT